PLAY CLAY

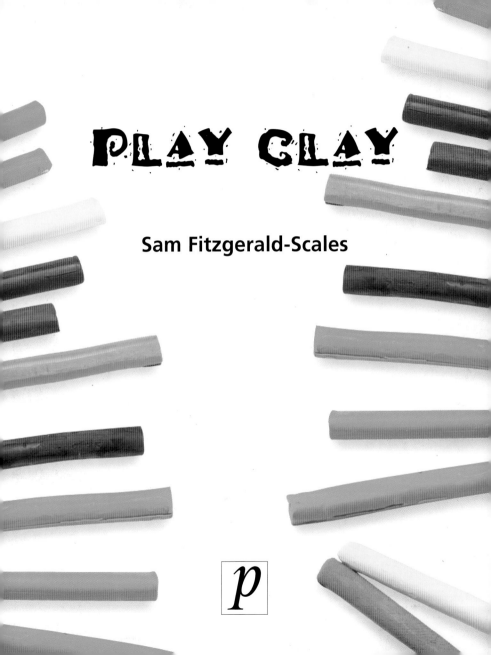

PLAY CLAY

Sam Fitzgerald-Scales

p

This is a Parragon Book

Parragon
Queen Street House
4 Queen Street
Bath BA1 1HE, UK

Designed, produced and packaged by
Stonecastle Graphics Limited

Text by Sam Fitzgerald-Scales
Designed by Sue Pressley and Paul Turner
Edited by Philip de Ste. Croix
Play clay models by Sam Fitzgerald-Scales
Photography by Roddy Paine
Styling by Sue Pressley and Paul Turner

ISBN 0-75256-277-0

Printed in China

DISCLAIMER:

- Play clay is great fun but safety is very important.
- Never put play clay in your mouth.
- Do not allow babies or young children under five years old to play with play clay as they may put it in their mouths and choke.
- Keep play clay away from family pets, who could swallow it and choke.
- Strong colours may stain fabric and other surfaces.
- Always wash your hands after using play clay.
- Always put your play clay away tidily and safely.

The publisher and their agents cannot accept liability for any loss, damage or injury caused.

CONTENTS

INTRODUCTION

C LAY HAS always fascinated me. There are endless possibilities when it comes to deciding what you are going to create, and whatever models you do make will almost certainly inspire you to experiment some more.

In this book I have chosen 28 projects for you to make, arranged according to their degree of difficulty. It is advisable to read the Helpful Hints on the opposite page first – they will tell you what you can use as tools and equipment to make it easier. There are also some tips on mixing your own colours!

As a potter and sculptor, I have used many different materials, but clay is my absolute favourite. The material that you are going to use is very similar to potter's clay, except that you do not need to bake it in a kiln.

I hope you will have hours of enjoyment creating all sorts of models, just as I do.

Remember, whatever you make will keep for as long as you want it, but the great thing about modeling clay is that, whenever you feel like it, you can simply roll it up and start all over again!

HELPFUL HINTS

A LL THESE projects are written in ascending order of difficulty – so we start with the easy ones and move on gradually to harder ones later in the book.

If you have not used any sort of modelling clay before, you might like to start at the beginning and work your way through the projects – in that way you will be well equipped to deal with the necessary techniques as they become more demanding.

You will not need many tools; these are the everyday items that you will require to tackle all the projects:

• Drinking straws • Blunt drawing pencil
• Teaspoon • Artist's paint brush
• Plastic knife • Cocktail sticks

The dye from modelling clay can be quite strong and it can penetrate many surfaces, so it is advisable to work on a plastic or wooden surface, such as a tray or an old chopping board, and not directly on a precious table top! It is also advisable to wear protective clothing so you do not spoil your clothes, and it's a good idea to wash your hands after using dark colours to prevent the colour staining lighter colours.

Don't forget that although modelling clay smells nice, and sometimes it even smells like sweets, it is not edible and must not be put in your mouth.

There are plenty of colours to choose from, but you can also mix your own. Here are a few tips. Adding white to a colour will make it paler, it makes black turn grey, and it makes red go pink.

Yellow + red = orange
Yellow + blue = green
Red + blue = dark purple

To make different greens, try adding different amounts of yellow or blue.

Have a go at mixing different colours together and see what you can come up with, but remember, if you mix too many together, you will simply end up with brown!

A SIMPLE SNAIL

WE WILL start by making a snail from two coils. You will find that coils are used for making many different projects, so the more you practise now in the early stages, the easier it will be to use them in various ways later on.

You can make differently sized snails once you have successfully made the first one. Try combining different colours together; for example, a brown body joined to a green shell with brown or yellow stripes.

2. On a flat surface roll two coils in different colours using the palms of your hands – keep them moving continuously to ensure an even shape. Cut them so that they are both about 13cm (5in) in length.

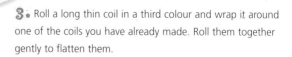

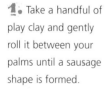

1. Take a handful of play clay and gently roll it between your palms until a sausage shape is formed.

3. Roll a long thin coil in a third colour and wrap it around one of the coils you have already made. Roll them together gently to flatten them.

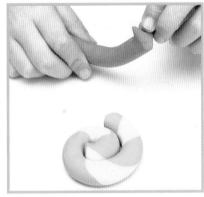

4. Starting at one end, roll the coil over onto itself until it is completely round.

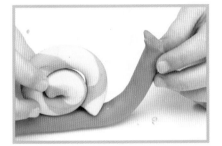

5. Gently squeeze one end of the coil to form a point for the tail. Carefully raise the other end so it is off the ground, then form two antennae by squeezing the clay tip between your fingertips.

6. Place this shape onto the middle of your remaining coil and press them together firmly to join the two pieces.

CHARMING SNAKE

LOTS OF people are afraid of snakes thinking they are all poisonous, but in fact many are completely harmless. At first glance they may not appear to be very attractive, but if you look closely they have beautiful patterns on their skin, which are made up of thousands of tiny scales. They look wet and slimy, but actually they are dry and cool to the touch because they are cold-blooded.

Choose whatever colours you like for this project; there are hundreds of snakes in the world that have brightly coloured skins, so you can let your imagination run wild.

2. To decorate the snake's body, roll a long thin coil in a contrasting colour and wrap it around the body in a spiral. Roll the two together to flatten them.

1. Roll out a long coil about 25cm (10in) long and 2cm (³/4in) thick. Round the head end off using your fingertips and roll the other end into a point.

3. Flatten the head slightly between your finger and thumb. Roll two black beads of clay and stick them on top of the head as eyes. Using a cocktail stick draw a line at the bottom of the head for the mouth.

4. Roll a short thin coil in red clay about 2.5cm (1in) long and pinch it into a fork at one end. This is the snake's forked tongue. Using a plastic knife, carefully cut into the mouth to open it out slightly, and then put the tongue inside.

5. Twist the model into upright position curling the snake onto itself. Make sure the bottom section is wider than the top so that it is stable and sits up securely.

CUTE CATERPILLAR

CATERPILLARS COME in many different colours and some are covered in fur – real hairy monsters! It is really easy to make this project, just follow the step-by-step instructions carefully and you will be delighted with the results.

1. Choose two different colours of modelling clay. Yellow, green, brown, black or white would be realistic colours, but feel free to choose whatever you like if you want something brighter. You can even mix colours together to make your own – see page 7 to find out how.

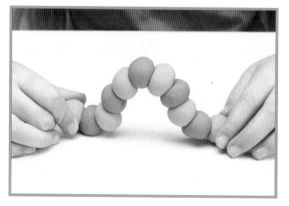

2. Break off five pieces of clay in each of your two chosen colours; they should be about the size of a marble. Roll them into balls in the palms of your hands until they are nice and round. They should all be the same size, or as similar as you can get.

3. Press the balls together one by one, forming an arch in the middle for its back.

4. Roll a slightly larger ball for the head and join it firmly to one end of the model. Using a teaspoon, push the end into the front of the head to form the mouth.

5. Roll two small beads of black clay for the eyes. Press and flatten them into position on either side of the head.

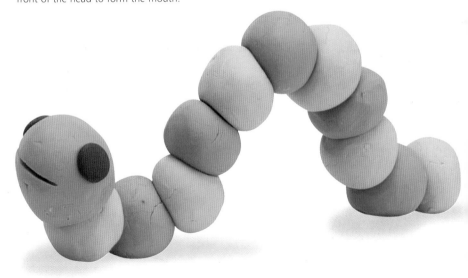

BUMBLE BEE

Even though they can sting, bumble bees are quite appealing, probably because the hair on their bodies looks like fur. They can have yellow and black or orange and black stripes. They have bulky rounded bodies and tiny wings in comparison. With such big bodies and small wings, they seem to defy the laws of science in being able to fly at all!

1. Take a small handful of black clay and roll it into a ball. Then roll it in the same direction a few times to elongate the shape slightly.

2. Roll a long thin coil about 10cm (4in) long in either orange or yellow clay.

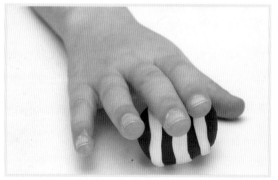

3. Carefully wrap the thin coil around the body of the bee leaving a gap between the stripes.

4. Roll the whole thing gently to flatten stripes, but be very careful not to squash your shape too much.

5. Roll two small beads of clay in yellow or orange and press them on either side of one end, which will form the head. These will represent the eyes. Roll out several tiny beads in black and press them all over the eyes to simulate the lattice effect of the insect's eye. You should leave small gaps so that some of the background colour still shows.

6. The wings on a bee are transparent, so choose a colour which you feel works best. You could use one of the colours you have already used, or perhaps white or blue which have a more transparent look. Roll two small balls of clay and mould one end of each to form a tear-drop shape. Use the end of a straw to press a texture into each side. Press them carefully onto the body of the bee to join them securely.

LOVELY LADYBIRD

EVERYBODY LIKES ladybirds – they are pretty to look at and they eat nasty bugs in the garden. Normally they are red with black spots on their bodies, but some are yellow or white and black. Unlike some insects, they do not have long, hairy legs or a sting in their tails, so they really are rather nice to know!

2. Press it down gently to create half an egg shape.

1. Take a good handful of red clay and roll it into a ball. Then model it carefully into an egg or oval shape.

3. Using a modelling tool or cocktail stick, draw a line down the middle to mark where the wings meet.

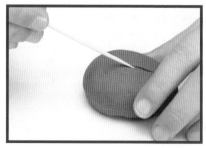

4. Flatten out a thin piece of black clay. Cut it into a semi-circle. Place this on one end of your shape to form the ladybird's head and trim it carefully into shape with a plastic knife.

5. Roll out small black beads of clay and press them on to the back to form the wingspots – three for each wing.

6. Roll two beads of white clay to form the eyes and press tiny black beads onto each eye for the finishing touch.

If you want to try making the yellow or white ladybird, follow the same steps but simply change the red clay for one of the other colours.

MIGHTY MOUSE

LOTS OF people are afraid of mice, probably because they scuttle about so quickly and dive under the nearest piece of furniture when surprised. But when you see them close up and they are still, they are really very cute, especially dormice with their exceptionally big ears.

Many children keep mice as pets – they take up very little space and they are great fun to watch. However, if you would prefer a clay mouse to a real one, try this cute model. Realistic colours to choose would be white, brown or black.

1. Take a small handful of clay and roll it into a ball. Roll it in one direction a few times to elongate it, then model the clay into an egg shape using your fingertips.

2. For the ears, roll out two small beads of clay about the size of a pea, using the same colour clay that you have selected for the body. Flatten them gently between your fingertips. Roll up two tiny beads of clay in pink and press them into the centres of these shapes. These will be the ears.

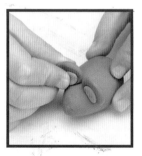

3. Gently press the ears onto the body at its smaller end, about a quarter of the way back.

4. Using a small straw, press it into either side of the head to form holes for the eyes. Roll two tiny beads of black or pink clay and press them into the centre of each eye.

5. Add another tiny bead of pink clay to the head for the nose.

6. Roll out a thin coil of clay about 2.5cm (1in) long, and attach it at the opposite end for the tail.

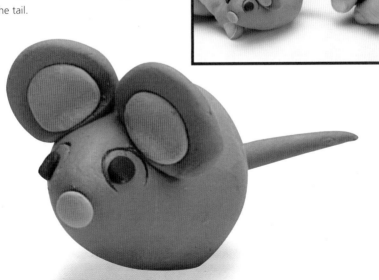

PORKY PIG

PIGS ARE great fun to make. They can be long and slim, or round and fat like the pot-bellied pig. They can be pink, or black, or both. Remember that the angle at which you place the ears gives the face its expression, so make two or three pigs and try out various options. Upright ears make them look alert, ears down look unhappy while ears back make them seem angry.

1. Take a small handful of clay and roll it into a ball using the palms of your hands working in a circular movement. Then roll it in one direction to elongate the shape. Using your fingertips, gently mould the clay until it is oval or egg-shaped.

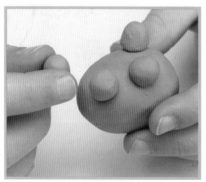

2. Roll seven small balls of clay each about the size of a thumbnail. Take five of them and roll each in one direction to form four legs and a snout. Roll the ends only of the two remaining balls of clay to form the ears, then flatten these out carefully between finger and thumb.

3. Join the legs to the body by pressing them firmly into position.

4. Add the ears and snout by pressing them firmly into place. Remember what I said about the ears influencing the expression of the pig.

5. Using the sharpened end of a pencil, press into the snout to form holes for the nostrils. Do the same for the eyes and then press small black beads in the centre.

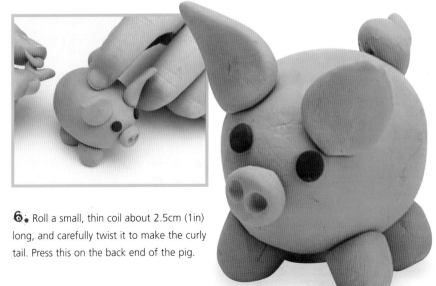

6. Roll a small, thin coil about 2.5cm (1in) long, and carefully twist it to make the curly tail. Press this on the back end of the pig.

AN ENGLISH ROSE

ROSES HAVE been grown in our gardens for a long time. Over the years, gardeners have cultivated new and different varieties: some have more petals, some have more powerful scent, some have fewer thorns. Some are small bushes and some grow tall almost like trees. There are hundreds of varieties to choose from these days.

The fragrance of each type of rose can be very distinctive and different coloured flowers produce different scents. Have a sniff next time you come across some and see which you like the best. Choose any colour you like for this project – perhaps the same colour as your favourite-smelling rose.

1. Take a small piece of clay and roll it into a small sausage shape in the palm of your hand. Flatten this with your fingertips evenly along the full length of the clay.

2. Carefully fold one end over and begin rolling it up, continue until the whole piece of clay is rolled. Then pinch one end.

3. Roll several small balls of clay and flatten them in the palm of your hand or pinch them into shape as shown above. Attach these one by one around the outside of the shape you have already made to form the petals. Bend them slightly into different shapes to make them look natural.

4. Roll a small ball of green clay, and then flatten one end in the palm of your hand to form a leaf shape. Using a cocktail stick, draw the veins of the leaf on both sides.

5. Stick the leaf to the outside of your rose as shown. You could make several roses in different colours and arrange them in a small bowl.

A BUNCH OF FLOWERS

THERE ARE many thousands of different types of flowers and they come in all sorts of shapes, sizes, and colours. Some are tiny, but some are very large, especially those that grow in hot countries where there is a lot of sunshine.

Next time you see some flowers, take a closer look at the detail – they are very delicate and perfectly formed. They are one of nature's miracles. I am going to show you how to make three different flowers, but you can experiment and create your own if you have more ideas. You can choose any colours you like for this project.

FIRST FLOWER

1. Roll a ball of clay in the palm of your hand and flatten it slightly. This is for the middle of the flower so perhaps you should choose orange or yellow which usually looks best.

2. Roll out six slightly smaller balls of clay in a different colour and press them around the edge of the centre piece that you have already made.

3. Roll out some tiny beads in another colour and press them around the centre.

SECOND FLOWER

1. Roll a ball of clay in the palm of your hand – again this is for the middle of the bloom.

2. Roll eight smaller balls of clay, moulding them at one end to form tear-drop shapes.

3. Press them around the edge of the centre piece.

4. Roll a long thin coil and wind it into a loose spiral – then press this onto the middle section.

THIRD FLOWER

1. Roll a ball of clay in the palm of your hand and shape it into a point at one end.

2. Roll out a few smaller balls of clay and flatten them in your palm.

3. One at a time, add these petals around the centre of the flower.

A FLATFISH

THERE ARE many varieties of fish. If you visit a pet shop you will find there are generally three different groups for keeping at home in a tank. First of all there are various kinds of goldfish which live in cold, fresh water. Secondly there are tropical fish which have to be kept in fresh water which is heated to make it warmer, and thirdly marine fish which are kept in salt water. Marine fish are the often most colourful, covered in brilliant rainbow colours.

Make your fish in bright colours to echo some of the wonderful fishes that thrive in the world's natural habitats.

1. Take a handful of clay and flatten it slightly. Then press it flat with the heel of your hand on a flat surface.

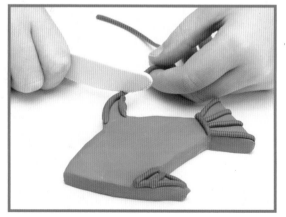

2. Using a plastic knife or a cocktail stick, cut out a fish shape. Carefully pick it up and smooth round the edges with your fingertips.

3. Roll out a very thin coil and cut it into strips – use this to make the shapes on the fins and tail. Trim off any excess clay with a knife.

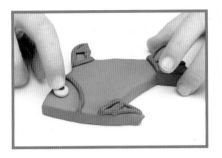

4. Use another strip to outline the head. Add a small ball of clay for the eye with a smaller black one for the pupil.

5. For the scales, roll about 16 small balls of clay, and, starting behind the head, press them down one at a time with your finger while dragging one end to create the shape of a scale. Cover the fish's body in this way row by row.

6. For the mouth, roll two very small balls of clay, one slightly larger than the other. Roll each one to a point at one end. Press them together and bend them slightly. Press this onto the lower part of the head as shown.

MORE FISHY BUSINESS

W E HAVE just seen how to make a flatfish – a fish in two dimensions, more like a tile or a wall plaque. Now we are going to make another type of fish. This one is three dimensional and will stand up on your table top when it's finished – very fishy!

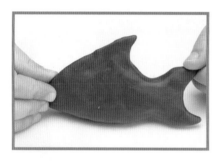

1. Take a handful of clay and roll into a fat sausage shape (but not too long).

2. Model it into a fish shape with a fin on the top. Leave it flat underneath so that it can stand up.

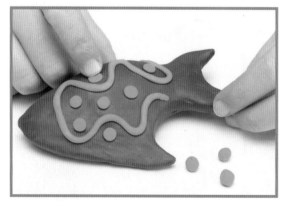

3. Roll out four long, thin coils in different colours and press them onto both sides of the body of the fish in wiggly lines. Roll tiny beads in another colour and stick them onto the body between the wiggly lines.

4. Roll out a long thin coil and cut it into strips. Add these to the fin and tail as shown, and trim with a plastic knife.

5. Roll two balls of clay, one bigger than the other, the smaller one in black. Flatten the larger one and add it to one side of the head for the eye, then press the black one in the middle for the pupil. Repeat on the other side for the second eye.

6. Add two short coils for the mouth.

BIRTHDAY CAKE

YOU CAN use whatever colours you like for this project, as cakes come in just about every colour that you can think of. Impress your friends on their birthday by handing them a miniature birthday cake that they can keep long after the real one has been eaten.

1. Roll two balls of clay in the palms of your hands, each about the size of a table tennis ball. Gently squash them down on a flat surface; you should end up with two 'burger' shapes.

2. Make a smaller ball in another colour and press it down on a flat surface to flatten it. This will be the 'cream' in the middle of the cake.

3. Place the 'cream' between the two flat pieces of clay.

4. Roll a second thin piece of clay and flatten in the same way. Cut an uneven edge with a plastic knife. Pinch the edges gently with your fingertips to give it a more finished look. This will form the icing. Place it on top of the cake.

5. Roll tiny beads of clay in a variety of colours and press them onto the top of the cake as decorations, just as you might put sweets on a real cake.

6. To make a candle, roll a short even tube about 2.5cm (1in) long. Make sure that the two ends are flat by tapping them on a flat surface, or by cutting them square with a plastic knife. Add a tiny pinch of yellow clay to the top for a flame. You can make as many candles as you like.

Good Enough to Eat

F OOD SPEAKS for itself; we all love to eat it! Everyone has a favourite meal. Adults often go for a traditional Sunday roast or an Indian or Chinese meal. Kids tend to love fast food like burgers; we all know that it is not very good for us to eat it all the time, but it tastes great!

I have chosen to make fried eggs, chips and peas, as it is popular with most people. The green peas add a nice touch of colour. You could make lots of different foods once you have got the hang of it.

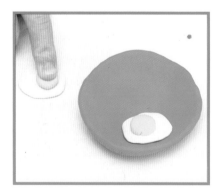

1. Take a handful of clay and flatten it into a burger shape. Using your fingertips model it into a simple plate-like shape lifting the edges slightly.

2. For the eggs, roll two small balls of white clay and flatten them gently. Roll two smaller yellow balls of clay for the yolks and press them into the centre of each egg white. Place them on your plate.

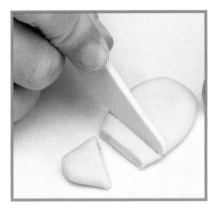

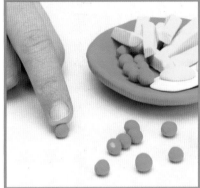

3. For the chips, roll out a piece of yellow clay with a rolling pin. Then use a plastic knife to cut it into strips and trim them to appropriate lengths. Add them to your plate.

4. For the peas, simply roll lots of little balls of green clay and scatter them on your plate, pressing them down slightly to make them stick.

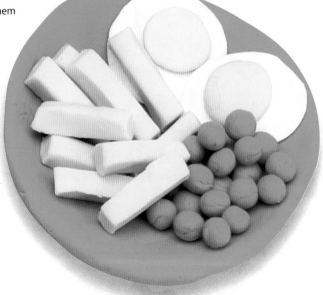

WOOLLY SHEEP

SHEEP CAN often be seen dotted around the countryside. Early in the year when all the spring lambs are born is the time when you will see them at their most interesting. Just like all baby animals, lambs are delightful to watch as they gambol around on their long legs while their mothers watch over them.

I have chosen to make a fully-grown sheep in this project as their thick woolly coats and round bodies are great fun to model.

1. Take a handful of white clay (or black if you are making a black sheep) and roll it into an egg shape in the palms of your hands.

2. Pinch out the shape of the head from the clay using your fingertips. Then in the same way pinch out the ears.

3. Roll four balls of black clay about a thumbnail in thickness, then roll them in one direction to elongate them into tubes. These will be the legs. Push the legs firmly onto the underneath of the body.

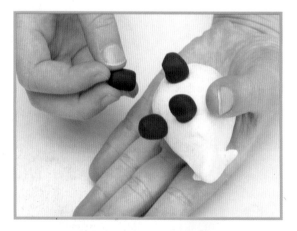

4. Roll several white balls of clay and stick them one by one all over the sheep's body to look like wool, leaving the head showing.

5. Add two tiny beads of clay in a contrasting colour for the eyes.

6. Roll two coils of black or brown clay and twist them to make horns. Roll a small ball of white clay and then shape one end of it to form a point. Flatten this slightly and add it to the back end of the sheep as the tail.

JACK RABBIT

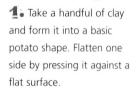

RABBITS AND their young can often be seen hopping around in the fields. Wild rabbits are normally brown in colour with a flash of white underneath their tails, which can be seen when they are running away into the distance.

Start by making the brown wild rabbit model shown here. You can then use your imagination and make a colourful pet rabbit with lop-ears.

1. Take a handful of clay and form it into a basic potato shape. Flatten one side by pressing it against a flat surface.

2. Carefully press down the sides of the shape towards one end with your fingertips to form the animal's hindquarters.

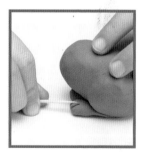

3. Roll four short, fat coils, and round them off neatly at one end. Press them underneath the body to make the feet.

4. Use a cocktail stick to mark out the toes.

5. Roll a ball of clay for the tail and squash it slightly between your finger and thumb, press it onto the back end of the rabbit. Add a thin white strip of clay underneath the tail. To make the head, roll a ball of clay and press it onto the front of the body and mould it into the head shape as shown.

6. Roll two coils about 2.5cm (1in) long, moulding each to a point at one end. Using your thumb, pinch along the middle of the shapes to form the ears. Press them onto the sides of the head, and bend one over to add a nice touch of expression.

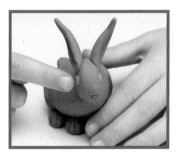

7. Add two tiny beads of clay in black or pink for the eyes. Mark out the nose and mouth with a cocktail stick.

TREVOR TORTOISE

TORTOISES ARE very prehistoric in appearance and they have an impressive life-span. They can live for over a hundred years, while giant tortoises are even more amazing – they can live for twice that length of time.

To make this model we shall use coils and balls of clay – shapes with which you should be quite familiar by now. The shell is made by pinching the clay – this is a great way of forming hollow shapes. Choose your colours carefully, using at least two different ones.

1. Take a handful of clay and roll it between your palms into a sausage shape.

2. On a flat surface, roll two coils about 10cm (4in) long and about a thumbnail thick and trim with a plastic knife.

3. Push them together – side-by-side and bend them slightly so that the two ends touch the ground. These will be the legs.

4. Make a ball of clay in the palms of your hands about the size of a table tennis ball. Push the thumb of one hand into the ball while it is lying in the palm of the other. Pinch it into a shallow bowl shape that is slightly oval.

5. Turn the bowl shape upside down and stick it onto the legs. Roll a small ball and model it into a head shape. Attach it to one end of the shell. Roll a small coil about 2.5cm (1in) long and pinch one end to a point. Attach this tail to the other end.

6. Roll six thin coils in a contrasting colour each about 13cm (5in) long and stick them onto the shell to form the typical pattern.

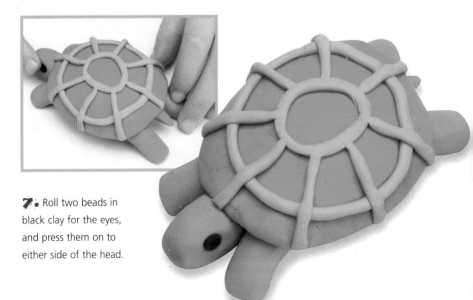

7. Roll two beads in black clay for the eyes, and press them on to either side of the head.

OLLIE OCTOPUS

OCTOPUSES ARE strange sea creatures. They have long arm-like tentacles that move gracefully through the water. Some of them grow very large and live at the bottom of the oceans; others can be quite small and are found in shallower waters, often in warmer climates.

You can be as creative as you like with colours here, so choose your favourites for this project.

1. Take a small handful of clay, roll it into a ball and then ease it into an oval. Mould it into the shape shown here, and flatten one side by tapping it on a flat surface.

2. Roll five coils each about 13cm (5in) long. Roll each end into a point and curl it over. These will be the tentacles.

3. Join three tentacles to the body at the places shown. Bend them into shape. Add the final coils in between the others.

4. Using a straw, press the end into the surface of the body and the tentacles to create an interesting texture.

5. Add tiny beads of clay over the whole body as extra decoration.

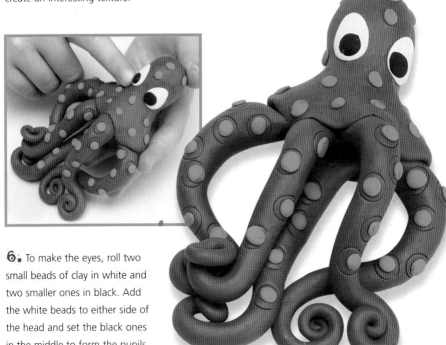

6. To make the eyes, roll two small beads of clay in white and two smaller ones in black. Add the white beads to either side of the head and set the black ones in the middle to form the pupils.

FROSTY THE SNOWMAN

S NOWY DAYS seem few and far between, so when that first flurry of snow starts to fall, we all hope there will be enough snow to make snowballs, go sledging and make a snowman. But whatever the weather, you can always make a snowman using modelling clay.

1. Roll two balls of white clay. One should be egg-shaped for the body, the other should be round and much smaller for the head. Put them together, but don't worry too much about the join as it will be covered by a scarf.

2. To make the scarf, roll a long thin coil in the colour of your choice, press it flat and add small pieces of clay in a contrasting colour for the stripes. Cut a fringe at each end of the scarf using a plastic knife or a cocktail stick.

3. Wrap the scarf around the snowman's neck – this will hide the join between the head and the body.

4. Roll two balls of clay in black or another dark colour. Flatten one for the brim and roll one into a marshmallow shape for the top hat. Join the two pieces and press onto the snowman's head.

5. Roll a small ball in orange and make it into a carrot shape for a nose. Add two tiny black beads of clay for the eyes and two slightly larger beads for the buttons. Make button-holes using a blunt pencil.

DELIGHTFUL DUCK

DUCKS ARE waterfowl that are frequently seen on ponds and lakes all around the countryside, and even in parks and gardens in towns and cities.

One particularly variety that you probably know well is the white farmyard duck. It is quite big and stands very upright. It has a bright orange beak and feet. Another familiar type is the mallard that we see mainly on ponds; their feathers are speckled browns and the male (called the drake) has a green shiny head.

1. Take a handful of clay and form it roughly into an egg shape.

2. Carefully mould the clay into a duck shape using your fingertips to pinch the clay.

3. Roll two small balls of orange clay for the feet, making one end of each ball slightly pointed. Flatten each at the base of the fatter end and press them to the underneath of the duck so that they stick out at the front

4. Make the head of the duck, which should be nice and rounded. Add two small black beads of clay for the eyes.

5. Roll two balls of white clay in the palms of your hands, and again form them to make a point at one end of each ball. Flatten them between your fingertips and press onto the sides of the duck to represent the wings.

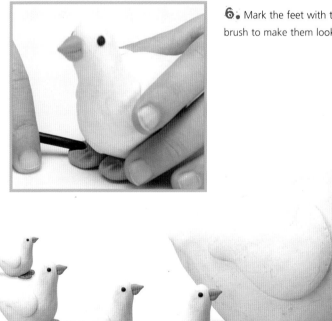

6. Mark the feet with the end of a paint brush to make them look webbed.

LITTLE LIZARD

LIZARDS ARE cold-blooded reptiles and they are generally found in hot countries where they bask in the sunshine to warm their bodies for energy. You may have startled one while out walking and seen how quickly it can scuttle away to safety.

Lizards range in size from small geckos to large dinosaur-like creatures called iguanas with high crested backs. The largest lizard in the world is called the Komodo dragon. This giant lives on the islands of Indonesia and can grow to be 3m (10ft) in length. It is big enough to kill and eat a deer!

Their colours in nature range from greys and browns to vivid greens and yellows. I have chosen green for this project, but you can use any colour.

1. Take a handful of clay and form a fat sausage. Press it flat with the heels of your hands.

2. Carefully cut out the lizard shape with a cocktail stick or a plastic knife. Cut a paper template to use as a guide if you find that easier.

3. Pick the lizard up carefully and smooth the edges with your fingertips.

4. Roll out tiny beads of clay in yellow and press them onto the toes as claws.

5. Roll a thin coil of clay in a contrasting colour. Measure the length of the body from behind the head to the end of the tail, and cut the coil to this size. Roll each end to a point and join it to the main body along the line of the backbone. Pinch between your finger and thumb along the coil.

6. Roll two small beads of clay and join to the head to form the eyes.

7. Add small green balls of clay to the back for decoration. Using the handle of a paint brush, push it into the spots to make indentations. Press a pencil into the nose to create the the nostrils.

COOL CATS

CATS ARE probably the most popular household pets these days. Their independence and ability to fend for themselves fit well with our busy lifestyles. They are fantastic athletes and can bend their bodies into the most amazing shapes.

I will show you how to make a standing and a crouching cat. Once you have successfully made these, you might like to try some different positions of your own.

1. Roll two coils about 18cm (7in) long and cut each end with a plastic knife.

2. Bend the coils into arches so that both ends touch the ground. Press both coils together as shown leaving them slightly apart at each end.

3. Roll a ball of clay about the size of a table tennis ball and flatten it slightly. This will be the head. Pinch out the ears, and model the chin to a slight point.

4. Form eye shapes in green or yellow clay and press them onto the face. Add small black beads for the pupils. Make a small triangle for the nose and scratch the mouth out using the end of a cocktail stick.

5. Roll a small coil of clay and make it pointed at one end for the tail. Attach this to one end of the body and the head to the other. Now you have a nice standing cat.

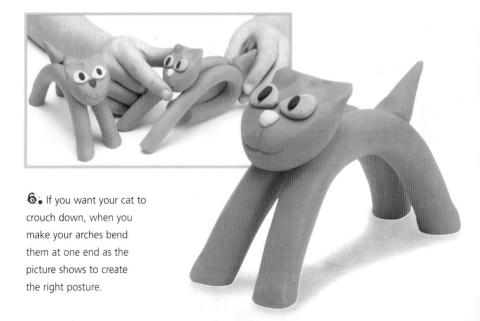

6. If you want your cat to crouch down, when you make your arches bend them at one end as the picture shows to create the right posture.

YOUR LITTLE PONY

P ONIES ARE smaller and often chunkier than horses. Because of their size, it is easier for children to learn to ride on them – there's not quite as far to fall! Realistic colours for this project would be black, white or brown, but a fantasy pony can be any colour you like and this is great fun to make.

1. Roll two coils about 18cm (7in) long and cut each end with a plastic knife.

2. Bend the coils into arches so that both ends touch the ground. These are the legs. Press both coils together leaving them slightly apart at each end, this will enable the legs to stand freely.

3. Roll a piece of clay into a small sausage shape in the palms of your hands. Bend the top part over and model a head and neck shape. Pinch out two ears.

4. Roll a coil about 5cm (2in) long and a thumbnail wide. Model this into a tail shape.

5. Roll two small beads of black clay for the eyes and stick them to either side of the head. Push the sharp end of a pencil into the end of the nose to make the nostrils.

6. Roll out several thin short coils with pointed ends and attach them along the length of the neck and between the ears to form the flowing mane.

7. Add the head to one end and the tail to the other, pressing them firmly into place.

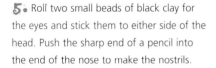

TEDDY BEAR

JUST ABOUT everybody has a soft spot for teddy bears; they are forever popular with children and seem never to go out of fashion. These days they have become very collectable, and people will pay a lot of money for antique teddy bears from particular manufacturers.

Most teddy bears are soft and squashy, but others can be firm and heavy depending on the material used for the filling. Bears made of other materials, such as pottery, are also popular with collectors.

1. This bear is basically made of nine different sized balls of clay. Study the picture and make all the sections as you see them illustrated ready to assemble. The arms and legs should be rolled in one direction a few times to elongate them and then flattened at one end.

2. Sit the body end up on a flat surface. Press the arms and legs onto the body.

3. Press the head onto the body; add the ears having first flattened them slightly.

4. Add the muzzle; round off the end and add a black bead of clay for the nose. Add two small beads of orange clay for the eyes; press two tiny black beads into the centres to form the pupils.

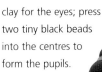

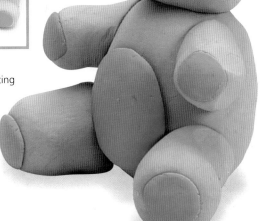

5. Roll four balls of clay in a contrasting colour, flatten them and add them to the ends of the arms and legs. Add a larger one in the same way to the tummy as shown.

DEADLY DINOSAUR

DINOSAURS HAVE fascinated children and adults alike for many years. It is hard to imagine that such huge creatures roamed the Earth many millions of years ago. Now is your chance to create your own dinosaur.

Once you have tried making this one, you can use your imagination to design new and original monsters.

We do not know what colours dinosaurs were in reality – they probably looked rather like lizards do today. So they may have been brown and green, or you could perhaps use blue, yellow and black. You are free to use whatever wonderful colours take your fancy!

1. Take quite a large handful of clay. Look carefully at the step-by-step photographs, and model the clay into the basic body shape shown. The bottom end must be pinched out to form a tail and the top rounded to form a head.

2. Take four more pieces of clay for the legs. Judge the amount of clay you will need by looking at the finished model. Mould the legs by using the photographs as a guide. The hind legs are much bigger than the front ones, which are in fact more like arms.

3. Press the legs onto the body shape; your model should now stand up with the hind legs firmly in place. Roll six small balls of clay into points to create the claws on the toes.

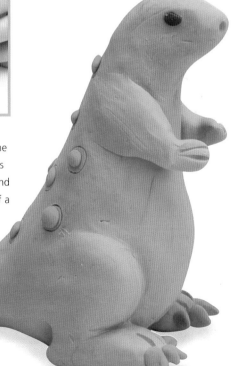

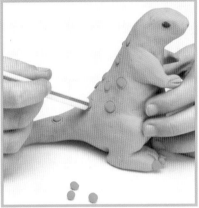

4. Add two tiny beads of clay to form the eyes. Add beads of clay to create the spots on the back and outline them using the end of a drinking straw. Press the sharp end of a pencil into the nose to create nostrils.

Finished? Now for Jurassic Park!

DANGEROUS DRAGON

THESE WONDERFUL creatures of myth and legend can be as strange and fanciful as you wish to make them. That goes for their colour too. Because they have never existed in the real world, we are free to make them just as we please. They can be scary or cute, spiky or smooth, pink or blue, winged or wingless – the choice is yours.

1. Using the same method as for the dinosaur, take a handful of clay and mould as much of the body shape as possible. This shape is less upright than the one we made for the dinosaur. Pinch the lower end to form a tail. Shape the other end to create the head and pinch out the ears.

2. Take four equally sized but smaller pieces of clay to model the legs. Attach these to the body and work the clay together to make a smooth join.

3. Roll a coil of clay in a second colour and add to the back from behind the ears to the end of the tail. Pinch down the length as shown in the photograph.

4. Add small spots or stripes using tiny beads of clay or small coils in different colours. Press them on to fix them in place.

5. Roll some small pointed pieces of clay in white for teeth and claws. Press them on in the appropriate positions. Pull the tail round to one side so that it curls towards the front.

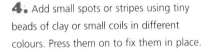

6. Add two tiny beads of black clay for the eyes. Press the sharp end of a pencil into the end of the nose to form the nostrils.

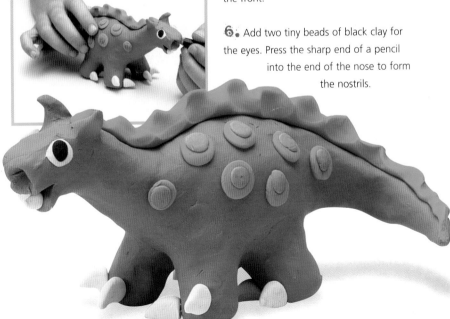

THE LION KING

THE LION is known as the king of the jungle and it is not hard to see why. Lions are big and powerful and very fast when hunting their prey. In fact, male lions can be quite lazy, leaving it up to the lionesses to provide the food. They live in groups called 'prides', and lions are the only big cats that hunt in groups rather than individually.

If you compare big cats with our domestic cats, you will see many similarities in their behaviour and in the way they move. Fortunately our little cats are not quite as dangerous!

1. Take a good handful of yellow clay and model it into the shape shown in the pictures. Using your thumb, mould the haunches on the body of the lion.

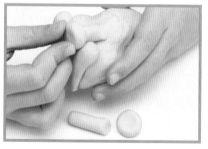

2. Roll a ball for the head and pinch a nose out using your fingertips. Press the head onto the body shape.

3. Roll two coils about 5cm (2in) long, and four balls of about thumbnail size. Add the coils to the front of the body for legs. Flatten the four balls; add two underneath the front legs, and two underneath the haunches for the paws.

4. Use the point of a cocktail stick to form the separate toes.

5. Roll out two small balls of clay and make the ears. Roll out several coils in orange clay. Make these pointed at one end. Add them to the head as shown to create the mane.

6. Add a brown triangle for a nose, and mark nostril and mouth lines with a cocktail stick or a pencil; add two black beads for the eyes.

7. Roll a long coil for the tail, add small orange coils with pointed ends to the end to form the tuft, and join this to the body.

COCO THE CLOWN

YOUNG CHILDREN love to see clowns dressed up in funny clothes and acting silly. And most grown-ups like it too! Clowns were originally associated with circuses, but these days we are just as likely to see them at children's parties or entertaining the crowds in theme parks.

This project gives you a chance to use all your favourite colours, as clowns' costumes are always very bright. Choose whatever combination you like.

1. Take a handful of clay for the body, a smaller one for the head, and two small ones for the arms. Then assemble the piece as you see in the photographs.

2. Roll out two black balls of clay for the boots and add these to the body. Press two coloured beads onto the top of each for decoration.

3. Flatten a piece of clay for the bow tie. Cut the shape out with a plastic knife. Roll a thin coil in the same colour clay and wrap it around the neck to complete the tie.

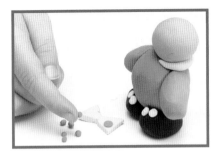

4. Roll out some small balls of clay and stick them to the tie to make the spots.

5. Join the tie under the chin. Add two or three small beads to the front of the costume for buttons. Use the sharp end of a pencil to press two holes in each button.

6. Roll out lots of small coils, twist them, and stick them to the head for hair.

7. Add two small beads for eyes, one for the nose and a red coil for the mouth.

JUMPING FROG

M OST OF us have seen frogs in ponds, under stones or at the zoo. For children, collecting frogspawn and watching tadpoles emerge and grow is always exciting. Amazingly, wherever a frog is born, it will return to that spot every year to produce its own spawn. It can be very confusing for them if the pond is not there anymore.

There are many different types of frogs; the brightest ones are found in hot countries and some of them are poisonous. For this model we shall choose a nice, harmless green frog.

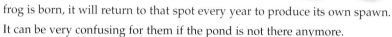

1. Take a handful of green clay and model it into the shape shown in the picture.

2. Roll two coils for the front legs and two smaller coils for the back legs. Make them all about a thumbnail in thickness with one end slightly thicker than the rest. Bend the two large legs in half and squeeze the middle into a point to form the knee as shown. Bend the two smaller front legs slightly.

3. Join the legs to the frog's body and press the feet flat. Using the handle of a thin paint brush, press three times into the feet to form the webs.

4. Add two small green balls of clay with black centres for the eyes. Mark out the nostrils with a cocktail stick or a pencil.

5. Add a few brightly coloured spots for decoration.

Now you can hop it!

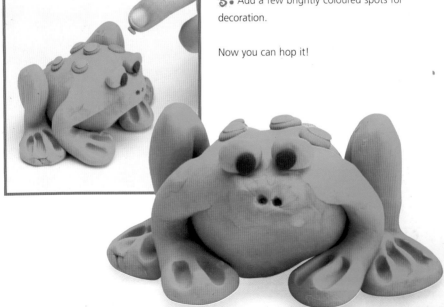

FURTHER INFORMATION

Once you have tried these projects and been bitten by the modelling bug, you will probably want to buy lots more clay to tackle even bigger projects.

Modelling clay can usually be purchased in most toy shops. It is available in a variety of colours.

There are also other types of modelling clay available in art and craft shops, such as air-drying clay or the type that hardens in the oven. When using these clays, once dry, the model can be painted and varnished.

If you decide to try one of these other clays, be sure to read the instructions as there may be differences in the way the material works, and in how it should be handled.

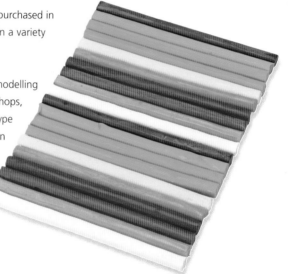